What are my jobs?

Bobbie Kalman

Crabtree Publishing Company

www.crabtreebooks.com

Created by Bobbie Kalman

Author and Editor-in-Chief
Bobbie Kalman

Educational consultants
Reagan Miller
Joan King
Elaine Hurst

Editors
Reagan Miller
Joan King
Kathy Middleton

Proofreader
Crystal Sikkens

Photo research
Bobbie Kalman

Design
Bobbie Kalman
Katherine Berti

Production coordinator
Katherine Berti

Prepress technician
Katherine Berti

Photographs
Marc Crabtree: cover (boy and dog),
    p. 3 (top left), 4, 5
Dreamstime: p. 6
iStockphoto: p. 10, 14 (left)
Shutterstock: cover (except boy and dog), p. 1, 3
    (except top left), 7, 8, 9, 11, 12, 13, 14 (right), 15

Library and Archives Canada Cataloguing in Publication

Kalman, Bobbie, 1947-
    What are my jobs? / Bobbie Kalman.

(My world)
ISBN 978-0-7787-9434-9 (bound).--ISBN 978-0-7787-9478-3 (pbk.)

    1. Chores--Juvenile literature. 2. Housekeeping--Juvenile
literature. I. Title. II. Series: My world (St. Catharines, Ont.).

TX301.K34 2010   j640   C2009-906096-5

Library of Congress Cataloging-in-Publication Data

Kalman, Bobbie.
    What are my jobs? / Bobbie Kalman.
        p. cm. -- (My world)
    ISBN 978-0-7787-9478-3 (pbk. : alk. paper) -- ISBN 978-0-7787-9434-9
(reinforced library binding : alk. paper)
    1. Home economics--Juvenile literature. I. Title. II. Series.

    TX148.K38 2010
    640--dc22

2009041212

Crabtree Publishing Company

Printed in China/122009/CT20091009

www.crabtreebooks.com   1-800-387-7650

Published in Canada
Crabtree Publishing
616 Welland Ave.
St. Catharines, Ontario
L2M 5V6

Published in the United States
Crabtree Publishing
PMB 59051
350 Fifth Avenue, 59th Floor
New York, New York 10118

Published in the United Kingdom
Crabtree Publishing
Maritime House
Basin Road North, Hove
BN41 1WR

Published in Australia
Crabtree Publishing
386 Mt. Alexander Rd.
Ascot Vale (Melbourne)
VIC 3032

Words to know

caring
for pets

cleaning
a room

making pizza

recycling

taking care
of baby

washing
clothes

My parents both work.
They do many jobs at home, too.
I help my parents by doing
jobs around the house.
I like caring for our pets.

I brush
the bunny.

I feed
the bird.

I give water to
the guinea pigs.

I train our dog.

I walk
the dog.

Sometimes, my room is a mess.
I need to clean it.
I pick up my books and toys
and put them away.

I pick up my dirty clothes and wash them.
I make my bed and clean the floor.
I like cleaning my room.

I am done.

I wash the vegetables for dinner.
I make a **salad** with some of the vegetables.

salad

My sister and I use the other
vegetables to make a **pizza**.
We add some cheese. Yum!

sink

After dinner, I help clean the kitchen.
I take the dishes to the **sink**.
I wash the dishes.
Tomorrow, it is my brother's turn to wash.

My job is to clean the kitchen floor.
I sweep the floor with a **broom**.
I sweep the dirt into the **dustpan**.
After I am done, I clean the table.

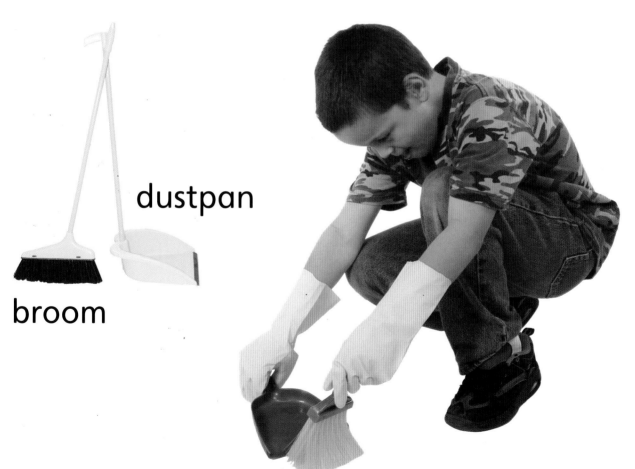

dustpan

broom

In the fall, I like to help outside.
My sister and I rake the leaves
in the yard with our father.
Soon, winter will come.
Then we will help shovel the snow.

We sort out the things that go
into our **recycling** bins.
We put plastic bottles into one bin.
We put cans into another bin.

What jobs do you do at home?
Jobs are more fun to do when
you listen to music and dance!

I dance and have
good clean fun.
I get the job done.

I like to wash the
car on a hot day.
It is cool fun.

I like to water our garden and cut the vegetables for dinner.

I like taking care of my dog.

I like washing and folding the towels.

I like taking care of the baby.

Notes for adults

What if?

What are my jobs? is a good introduction to the importance of work and promotes sensitivity to the work that parents do to look after a home and children. Ask the children to list the jobs around their homes. Write the jobs on the board. Which jobs are done by parents or other adults? What would be the consequences of not doing the following jobs—laundry, washing dishes, cooking meals, taking out garbage, recycling, or cleaning the home. Would children be happy if these jobs were not done?

How can children help?

Children could practice the above jobs in the classroom. They could learn to sort the recycling, wash and dry some plastic dishes, clean the classroom, and prepare some food in the class. (Note: The child on page 8 is cutting a tomato. Is she paying careful attention to what she is doing? How could she do this more safely? Could she use a plastic knife with a serrated edge? Using this picture, brainstorm kitchen safety with your students.)

Making it fun

Doing jobs empowers children and teaches responsibility. It can be a lot of fun, too! Before cleaning a home or classroom, a parent or teacher can write the names of jobs that need to be done on pieces of paper. Each paper describes one job. The papers are then put into a hat or other container. Each person chooses one job at a time, until all the job papers are gone. There should be an equal number of papers for everyone involved. Then, turn on some lively music and have some good "clean" fun!